Contents

Any words appearing in the text in bold, **like this**,
are explained in the Glossary.

Town and city habitats

A **habitat** is a place where plants and animals live. The towns and cities of the British Isles were built for people to live in and they seem, at first glance, to be totally unsuitable for wildlife. In fact, there is a huge variety of plants and animals in our towns and cities and these **urban** areas are becoming increasingly important wildlife habitats.

Get this!

Although only about 10 per cent of England's land is covered with towns and cities, almost 90 per cent of people live in them.

Adapting to urban life

As the population of the British Isles has grown, so people have cleared more woodlands and other wild areas to make room for towns and cities. Some of the animals that lived in those wild areas have **adapted** to urban life in order to survive. For example, many bats in the past would have lived in caves or in woodland. Today, they live in roofs of buildings.

Towns and cities can be surprisingly green areas, with tree-lined streets that supply food and shelter to many different animals. ➔

A variety of habitats

The food that people drop and throw away in towns and cities attracts many animals. Towns and cities also provide plants and animals with a range of different habitats. As well as the more obvious green areas, such as parks and gardens, there are neglected cemeteries, abandoned buildings and railway embankments. Many urban wildlife areas are linked together by railway lines, canal towpaths and hedgerows that allow animals to move around safely.

Living together

The lives of the plants and animals in a town or city are closely bound up with each other. For example, the colourful butterflies that fill our gardens in summer rely on plants for food and somewhere to lay their eggs. Many plants in turn rely on butterflies to **pollinate** their flowers.

← This map shows the main towns and cities of the British Isles.

Life in the streets

City streets and buildings are perhaps the hardest places to imagine wildlife living, but many plants and **insects** make their homes on our pavements, walls and homes.

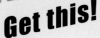

Get this!

Trees are often called the lungs of a city. They take in **carbon dioxide** and release **oxygen** during photosynthesis, and help to reduce air pollution.

Plants and pollution

One of the challenges facing **urban** plants is **pollution**. Grime and exhaust fumes from vehicles coat the leaves of plants and reduce **photosynthesis**. Some plants such as holly and ivy cope with this pollution because they have a protective **waxy** coating on their leaves.

Soil challenges

Another challenge for living things in towns and cities is the lack of soil. **Lichens** do not have roots – they take in **nutrients** from rainwater. This means they can survive in little or no soil. Some plants such as ivy have roots in the soil, but climb using tiny roots that grow from their stems into cracks in walls.

Plants that grow between paving slabs, such as dandelions and grasses, grow from seeds that blow into the narrow spaces. ➜

Insects

Large numbers of black ants live together in nests, which they make under pavements or in gaps at the base of a wall. Ants do well in cities because they can live off tiny scraps of leftover food. They locate food using their **antennae**. Wasps follow the scent of sweet leftover food in bins or houses. Wasps usually nest in tree holes, but in cities they also build their papery nests in attics and roofs.

Houseflies find food in kitchens or bins by smelling it with their antennae. They feed by coughing up stomach juices on to the food to make it liquid. Then they suck it up with their funnel-shaped mouth. Houseflies are **pests** because they carry germs and sometimes lay their eggs on food.

Life on a wall

In among the plants that grow on a wall is a natural world in miniature. The plant leaves and stems provide shelter for numerous insects, spiders and snails from bad weather and from bird **predators**. These small animals also use the stems of climbing plants, such as ivy, to climb the wall. Snails graze on plant leaves and use calcium, a chemical in the stone of walls, to build their shells. This wall has pennywort, Kenilworth ivy and Mexican fleabane plants growing on it.

Other animals in the streets

For birds and **mammals** that can cope with the disturbances caused by people and traffic, there are advantages to living in a city. For example, in winter, cities are warmer than the countryside because heat escapes from buildings and machines. There may also be fewer wild **predators**.

Bird life

Some birds, such as house sparrows, live in city **habitats** all year round. Although some starlings live in the British Isles, others only move in over winter to avoid cold weather elsewhere. They often group in flocks of hundreds, perching on buildings or city trees. Tawny and little owls perch on lampposts, looking out for sparrows and mice to eat.

Pigeons are one of the most common birds in towns and cities. They nest on ledges of buildings and fly down to eat food scraps. ➘

Many birds, such as pigeons and herring gulls, are **scavengers**. They eat whatever food scraps they can find dropped on the streets. Crows often patrol kerbsides looking for small animals killed by traffic to eat.

Urban mammals

Many **urban** mammals are **nocturnal**. They come out at night when there are fewer people and less traffic about, and they cannot easily be seen. Pipistrelle bats spend the daytime in roofs of churches and attics. At night they feed on the many **insects** that fly around city streets, attracted by the lights. A pipistrelle bat can eat 3000 insects in one night!

Rodents, such as brown rats and house mice, have very sharp front teeth. Their teeth help them bite through and eat almost anything, from food stored in cupboards to soap or even cardboard! The house mouse, as its name suggests, often lives beneath floorboards or behind walls of houses. House mice have good hearing and at night use their whiskers feel their way around.

Brown rats

If you see an animal about the length of a recorder, with short legs and long tail, scurrying across a street at night, it is probably a brown rat. Brown rats first arrived in Britain in the 18th century on ships from Norway. They are now the commonest rodents in Britain. They often live in sewers under city streets, emerging on to streets to feed at night.

Oxford city centre

Like many major cities, Oxford is full of buildings and people, but also has a variety of wildlife living amongst them. Some wildlife lives in **habitats** such as churchyards and even traffic islands.

↑ This map shows the Oxford city centre. The most important roads are shown in red.

Churchyards

Churchyards are quiet places where many animals rest and feed. St Mary Magdalen and Holywell cemeteries in Oxford both contain yew trees. These are dark green trees with flat needle-shaped leaves. Birds, such as mistle thrush, eat the flesh of red yew berries and spit out the poisonous seed within. Other birds, such as wrens, hop through the dark yew undergrowth looking for spiders and other animals to eat.

Ivy and **lichens** grow on gravestones in many churchyards. Ivy flowers appear in autumn and **insects**, such as hoverflies, feed on their **nectar**.

Mistletoe

Mistletoe grows on many trees in Oxford. Mistletoe gets its **nutrients** from tree branches – it is a tree **parasite**. Its sticky seeds start to grow on the branches when birds wipe them off their beaks after eating mistletoe berries.

↗ More lichens grow on rough surfaces of older gravestones than the polished marble of newer ones.

Oxford foxes

Foxes are commonly seen in **urban** habitats because there is lots of food to be found. They sniff out food, such as chicken bones and leftover takeaways, in dustbins, compost heaps, or in gutters. Waste food like this requires less energy to get than catching live **prey** and it is available year-round. However, urban foxes also dig up earthworms to eat and even catch birds, such as pigeons.

Foxes live in different parts of the Oxford city centre. Some are regularly seen in the quiet surroundings of Holywell cemetery. Other foxes are often seen at night on a grassy traffic island in Oxford called The Plain. They even started to build an earth (den) there.

Urban fox earths

Foxes make earths or burrows to have their cubs in. In the countryside, each female usually makes her own earth, but in urban places it is common for two females to share an earth and rear two litters of cubs. This is because there are fewer suitable patches of soil to dig earths in.

Urban foxes often knock over dustbins to steal leftover food. ↓

Parks and gardens

Parks and gardens can provide mini versions of natural **habitats**, such as woodland and hedgerow. They are also busy with people, including picnickers, playing children and gardeners.

Plants

The colourful flowering plants gardeners choose, such as roses, geraniums and peonies, have bright petals and sweet scents. These attract bees and other **insects** to feed on their **nectar** and help **pollinate** the flowers. Many favourite garden flowers are not **native** to the British Isles. They were brought from countries far away in the past. For example, rhododendrons were brought from Southeast Asia. Park and garden trees, including horse chestnut, wild cherry and holly, provide shade for people and food and shelter for many insects, birds and other animals.

Grass

Grass is ideal for lawns in parks and gardens because it is tough enough to withstand being trampled. It also grows back quickly after being mown because, unlike most plants, it grows from its base instead of its leaf tips.

There are about half a million hectares of garden in Britain, with half as much land again in public gardens and parks! ➜

Park and garden pests

Gardeners consider many insects and other small animals to be **pests**. Aphids or greenfly are small bugs that reproduce quickly – each female can give birth to 50 young in her 3-week life. They suck up **sap** from inside plants, such as roses, using their straw-shaped mouth. When their numbers build up, they can destroy plants. Slugs are pests that glide around on a trail of slime at night, nibbling leaves.

Gardeners' friends

Some animals, such as ladybirds and earthworms, are gardener's friends. A ladybird is a kind of spotted beetle that eats aphids. Earthworms swallow bits of earth, and extract tiny bits of food from it as it passes through their body. This helps gardeners by making soil finer and putting **oxygen** into it, which helps plants to grow.

Get this!

Ladybirds are brightly coloured to warn birds not to eat them – they release a nasty-tasting liquid from their legs if attacked!

◤ Living among garden grass, plants and soil are hundreds of different kinds of small animals.

Animals in parks and gardens

Parks and gardens provide a variety of places for birds and **mammals** to live or take shelter. They also become valuable sources of food. The greatest threat to **urban** birds is pet cats, which kill millions of birds a year. You can help by tying a bell to your cat's collar, to warn birds when it approaches!

Garden birds

Many park and garden birds, such as house sparrows and greenfinches, feed on seeds. Some birds, such as blackbirds and song thrushes, search lawns and flowerbeds for earthworms and snails. Robins often perch nearby when gardeners work, waiting for worms and beetles to be dug up. Some park and garden birds feed on the **insects** and moths that visit flowering plants to feed on **nectar**. Wrens are tiny birds that clamber over garden walls and sheds, or among climbing garden plants such as clematis searching for spiders to eat. Some larger birds, such as magpies, feed on the eggs and chicks of other birds.

Many urban animals eat a variety of food. These blackbirds are making a meal of a windfall apple in a city garden. ↓

Park and garden mammals

Many park and garden **mammals** keep out of the way of people during the day. Foxes may lie up beneath garden sheds, while hedgehogs rest under hedges or piles of leaves. Hedgehogs are popular with gardeners because they eat many of the slugs, beetles and insect **larvae** that feed on garden plants. Shrews have a similar diet. These small **rodents** use their long snout to smell out **prey** in the dark and they often dig up their food.

Moles live in underground tunnels and feed on earthworms and other small animals that fall into the tunnels. Moles are considered **pests** by gardeners because they can push the soil they dig up to the surface of lawns in piles called molehills. Molehills spoil the look of a smooth lawn.

↑ Hedgehogs have 36 small sharp teeth to crunch their food.

Grey squirrel

Unlike many urban mammals, grey squirrels feed during the day. They can often be seen bounding amongst trees in parks and gardens. Grey squirrels are not **native** British mammals. People brought them from America over 100 years ago. They thrive in towns and cities because they eat a wide range of foods. Grey squirrels not only eat acorns, nuts, fruit and flowers from trees, they also **scavenge** food leftover by people in bins.

City lakes and ponds

The ponds and lakes in parks and gardens around the British Isles are important wildlife **habitats**. Animals, such as foxes and hedgehogs, come to drink at the ponds, and the plants that grow there provide food and shelter for many other animals.

At the bottom of the pond

Many animals live in the mud at the bottom of a pond. Freshwater mussels filter the water they pass through their shells for tiny bits of food. Newts lie in wait to catch small fish. **Insect larvae** and worms eat decaying plant and animal matter that sinks to the bottom. Flatworms glide over the mud, eating small insects.

On the surface

Insects, such as whirligig beetles and pond skaters, skate lightly over the water's surface in ponds and lakes. They feed on insects that fall into the water. Pond snails use surface tension to hang on to the underside of the water, and move across it to find **algae** to eat. Mosquito and midge larvae also hang below the surface, feeding on tiny water animals that pass by. These larvae turn into flying adults that are hunted by other insects. Dragonflies catch flies in their powerful hooked jaws.

↑ Pondskaters find food by sight, or by sensing slight vibrations on the water's surface.

In the water

Water spiders breathe underwater by carrying an air bubble with them. They feed on insect larvae and are eaten by fish and frogs. Goldfish hide and swim among pond plants that they eat. Other fish, such as perch and sticklebacks, eat small animals, such as shrimps, which feed on algae and other tiny plants.

At the edge

Some birds make their nests among the plants at the edge of ponds and lakes. Mallards, geese and swans dive, or dip underwater to feed on plants there. Wading birds, such as herons, stalk the edges of ponds hunting fish and frogs.

Get this!

Over 80 per cent of all ponds in the British Isles are in gardens or school grounds.

Amphibians

Frogs and toads are **amphibians**. They hatch into tadpoles from eggs laid in water. This picture shows tadpoles of the common frog. As tadpoles they eat bits of underwater plants with tiny teeth, and breathe through special parts called gills. When they become adults they develop lungs and move on to land where they use their long sticky tongues to catch insects, slugs and other small animals.

Holyrood Park, Edinburgh

Holyrood Park in Edinburgh, Scotland covers 260 hectares of land and includes three lochs (lakes). Many different plants and animals live here, including some of the rarest **species** in Scotland. These include the blind white snail, a tiny snail that lives underground, and flowering plants such as the sticky catchfly.

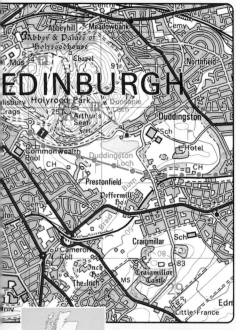

↑ This map shows Holyrood Park in Edinburgh, and the locations of Arthur's Seat and Duddingston Loch within it.

Arthur's Seat

The centre of the park is Arthur's Seat, a hill that is the remains of an old volcano. The pink-flowered sticky catchfly grows on rocky ledges here. It is misnamed because it does not catch flies – the sticky hairs on its stems stop **insects** crawling up and stealing its **nectar**!

Duddingston Loch

The area around Duddingston Loch is a rich **wetland** with 130 different kinds of wetland plants. Along one edge of the loch there is a band of marshland with reeds, willow trees and poplar woodland. Many birds, including great crested grebes, tufted ducks and swans, **breed** here among the dense plants. **Birds of prey**, such as kestrels and sparrowhawks, hover above the ground seeking **prey** including other birds and **rodents**.

Geese and ducks feed, breed and shelter in and around Duddingston Loch. →

Mammals of Holyrood Park

Among the **mammals** found in Holyrood Park are otters, which hunt for fish and frogs within the water. At night bats fly around the trees catching insects. Voles, rabbits and brown hares live in burrows under the grassy hills and fields of the park. Rabbits and brown hares eat mainly grass, while voles also eat fruit, seeds and snails. These three mammals are prey for two of the park's most successful hunters – stoats and weasels.

Get this!

There are more trees in Edinburgh than in the surrounding countryside!

Stoats and weasels

Stoats (like the one in the picture here) and weasels have a long, slim body, a pointed muzzle (snout), short legs and a long tail. They have a chestnut or chocolate-brown back and pale belly. Stoats are usually larger than weasels and have a black-tipped tail. Stoats eat mainly rabbits, but also ground-nesting birds and small rodents. Weasels are so slim they can chase their prey into their underground burrows to catch them. Stoats and weasels can be active day or night, and they rest in holes among tree roots or in abandoned burrows.

In winter, stoats in the north of Britain turn white – except for a black tip to their tail – to **camouflage** them against snow. Stoats further south, where it is less snowy, stay brown all year.

Wasteland

In nearly every town or city in the British Isles there are patches of land that people no longer use called wasteland. Wasteland includes land around disused railways, canals or factories, demolished buildings, waste tips, and old cemeteries. People in the past cleared these areas of wild plants and animals to provide houses, transport or work for growing town and city populations. When people stopped using the land, different plants and animals soon started to live on it. Wasteland is now an important **urban habitat** for wildlife.

Colonization

Colonization is when living things start to live on uninhabited land. Wasteland soil is often low in **nutrients** or full of rubble, such as broken bricks, so only certain things can live there. The first colonizers are plants. Tiny **spores** of mosses and ferns blow into cracks on walls and start to develop into new plants. Plants, such as rosebay willowherb, dandelion and thistle, are next to colonize the bare ground. Their seeds are light and covered in hairs that act as parachutes. They may be blown for miles before they land.

Plants and animals take over wasteland until it is disturbed once more by people. ↓

Wasteland succession

The types of plants on wasteland change over time. Many of the early colonizers of bare soil are annuals, such as poppies. Annuals grow rapidly from seed in spring and summer, make their own seeds and then die in autumn. As annuals cover the bare land, other plants gradually start to grow.

Some plants, such as grasses, grow from wind-blown seeds. Others, such as brambles, grow from seeds dropped by birds. These are perennial plants. Once perennial plants are established they live for several years. Eventually, a few tough shrubs, such as gorse, and trees, such as elder, may establish. This natural change in plants over time is called succession.

Butterflies uncoil their long tube-shaped mouth or **proboscis** to reach the nectar in buddleia flowers.

The butterfly bush

Buddleia is a typical wasteland plant. It bears long spikes of purple or white flowers with a strong perfumed scent. This advertises a rich supply of **nectar** to a wide range of butterflies and other insect **pollinators**. Buddleia grows from a winged seed into a large shrub in just a few years. It can establish anywhere from open soil to a moist crack in a chimney.

Wildlife in wastelands

Plants are vital to **urban habitats**. They provide food, shelter and a place to **breed** for many types of animals. The following birds and animals feed on wasteland plants.

Wasteland bugs

Bugs are beetles that suck **sap** from the stems of plants using their **proboscis**. Aphids, shield bugs and froghoppers live on wasteland plants, such as rosebay willowherb. Young froghoppers make bubbly froth around themselves, called cuckoo spit. This allows them to feed out of sight of most **predators**.

Lizards

Common lizards and slow worms are **reptiles** that often live on quiet wasteland with patches of bare ground. Slow worms are unusual lizards without any legs. They often slither through long grasses at dusk hunting slow-moving **prey**, such as worms and slugs.

↑ Common lizards often bask in sunny spots of bare ground on wasteland.

Cinnabar moths

Cinnabar moths lay their eggs on common ragwort on wasteland. Ragwort contains poison that harms many animals, but not cinnabar caterpillars. They build up the poison in their bodies so they taste bad to predators. The caterpillars' yellow and black stripes warn birds to leave them alone!

Many reptiles hatch from tough-skinned eggs laid on land. A female common lizard does not lay eggs. Her young develop fully inside her body. They are born in special skin sacks in sheltered spots during summer.

Birds and mammals

Many birds and **mammals** on wasteland are visitors in search of food. Goldfinches flock around teasels in autumn. They use their pointed beaks to carefully pull out seeds to eat from its spiky flowers. Other birds, such as pied wagtails and starlings, search for beetles amongst wasteland plants.

The strips of wasteland bordering railways often link town and city habitats with the countryside in the British Isles. Different **mammals**, such as badgers, foxes and brown rats, use these 'green highways' to move around.

Rubbish tips

Rubbish tips are a rich habitat for many animals. They provide an easy source of food, warmth from rotting rubbish and shelter. Flies eat and lay eggs on rotting food, cloth and paper. Worms thrive in the moist, rich soil. Birds, such as herring gulls, wait to eat leftover food, worms and insect **larvae** unearthed by giant diggers moving the rubbish around. Foxes sometimes make permanent dens sheltered amongst old tyres or cars where they rear their cubs.

Battersea Power Station, London

Battersea Power Station was built in 1936 to provide electricity for London. The massive brick building lies within a network of rail tracks. For nearly 50 years, trains brought in millions of tonnes of coal to burn in the station. Battersea Power Station and its tracks were closed in 1983. Although small parts have been redeveloped, it remains the largest single area of wasteland **habitat** in Europe.

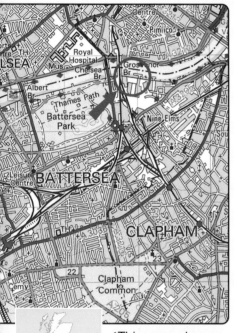

↑This map shows the location of Battersea Power Station in London. The waterway running across the map is the River Thames.

Station life

London rocket is a small plant with yellow flowers and long seed pods found at Battersea. As the pods dry, they twist open, scattering seeds around. London rocket is actually from the Mediterranean. It was accidentally brought to the British Isles during World War I. London rocket, along with Oxford ragwort and other plant invaders, probably arrived at the power station by railway. When plants along railways produce seeds, new plants sprout nearby. Over time, **species** gradually move along rail tracks into new areas.

↑ A buddleia bush grows on the edge of wasteland in the shadow of the giant chimneys of Battersea Power Station.

Power station birds

Some birds, such as house sparrows, **breed** on the wasteland here, making nests in walls or dense shrubbery. The scattered low plants and bare ground supply lots of **insects** and seeds to eat. Power station buildings, rusting cranes and other tall objects built by people offer sheltered nest sites that are well off the ground.

Birds of prey come to live and breed around the power station. They feed on the smaller wasteland birds. Peregrine falcons catch and eat pigeons and other birds with their sharp claws and hooked beak. Female peregrines lay eggs on high brick ledges at Battersea Power Station. The male peregrine feeds the chicks on pieces of meat it rips from its **prey**.

Get this!

Peregrine falcons are among the fastest birds on earth. They can dive at speeds up to 180 kilometres per hour in pursuit of their prey!

Black redstarts

A flash of black and red at Battersea might be a black redstart. They are black birds with red tails that originally came from mountainous parts of southern Europe. Although they are rare over most of the British Isles, they are common around Battersea Power Station. Black redstarts live and breed among the buildings here, and feed on the insects.

25

Seasons in a city

In winter there are fewer hours of daylight and it is colder. Birds such as gulls **migrate** in winter from the coast to cities, where it is warmer. During winter people leave food out in parks and gardens for some animals to feed on, but many animals have trouble finding enough to eat. As many plants die back in winter, there is less food for **herbivores**. This means that there are fewer herbivores in parks and gardens so there is fewer **prey** for **carnivores**.

This **food web** shows how animals in an urban **habitat** are linked together. Plants are producers – they harness energy from the Sun in the process of **photosynthesis** and make their own food. Animals are consumers – they eat plants and/or animals. ↓

Surviving cold winters

Many animals survive winter by avoiding it! In some **insect species**, such as aphids, all adults die in winter. Before that they lay eggs on plants that will hatch in spring as soon as it starts getting warm. Many other **urban** animals **hibernate** – they go into a deep sleep. Their body processes (such as breathing) slow down so they use less energy, and do not need to eat. Earthworms and slugs burrow deep into the ground to escape the frost.

Ladybirds and other beetles hibernate in walls or under tree bark. Butterflies spend the winter in dark corners of houses and garages. Hedgehogs hibernate under piles of leaves in gardens. Many pond animals sink to the bottom and spend the winter there, away from the freezing surface waters.

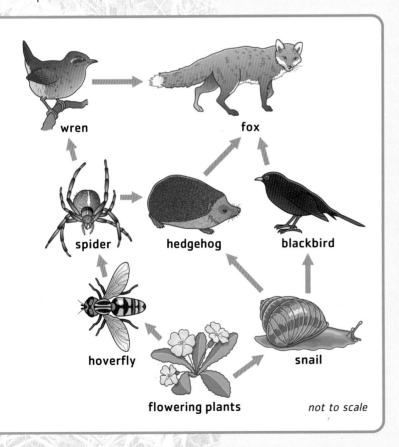

wren   fox

spider   hedgehog   blackbird

hoverfly   snail

flowering plants   *not to scale*

Spring and summer

In spring and summer it is sunnier and warmer and there are more hours of daylight. Plants burst into life and their flowers open. Insects hatch from eggs, and butterflies awaken to feed on flower **nectar**. Most animals have their young in spring and summer as it is warmer and there is more food about. Many urban animals, such as swifts and red admiral butterflies, are summer visitors to the British Isles.

← Summer is the season when things get really busy in parks and gardens. With more people around, wild animals are more likely to be disturbed.

House martins

If you see a cup-shaped mud nest just under the edge of your roof in summer, the chances are you have a family of visiting house martins. House martins have a white belly, with black wings and tail and a black cap. The parents fly above catching insects. They return to the nest every few minutes to feed their young until they are ready to fly and hunt themselves.

Who cares about urban habitats?

Town and city **habitats** – and the wildlife that depends on them – face many threats in the British Isles. Most come from the increasing populations in **urban** places. More people need more houses to live in, and areas such as wasteland are some of the only remaining spaces to build on.

The problems of city nature

People do not want certain types of wildlife such as rats, ants, cockroaches or woodworm in places they live, work or eat. This is because they can harm people or their pets, or damage buildings. However, the chemicals people use to get rid of these creatures can sometimes harm helpful animals such as bees, spiders and bats.

More people also create more **pollution**. If the air is badly polluted in a city, some plants can no longer survive there. Waste can pollute ponds, canals and wasteland. Vandalism is another problem. Some people intentionally damage trees and other plants in parks and gardens.

The value of city nature

The plants and wildlife in cities can make us feel good. For example, when daffodils bloom in a park they are beautiful to look at. They also remind us that spring has arrived. More importantly, trees and other plants improve our health. We need the oxygen they make through **photosynthesis** to breathe. Trees also help reduce traffic noise and pollution, and provide shade from sunlight.

↑ Rubbish can pollute and ruin city ponds like this one in Oxfordshire.

How do people help?

Many people try to improve urban habitats for wildlife. **Conservation** groups sometimes buy wasteland or disused allotments. They dig ponds, and plant hedgerows and trees to attract wildlife. Volunteers help clear up dumped waste in ponds and other habitats. Town councils plant more trees alongside roads and railways. Gardeners plant **nectar**-rich plants, such as buddleia, or put bird food out in winter to attract animals to their gardens.

Deptford Creek, London

Deptford Creek is a muddy stream that flows into the River Thames in London. Conservation workers have stopped it being used as a dump and tidied up to encourage wildlife. Now, grey herons feed and kingfishers nest there and a varied mix of plants grow on the wooden flood defence walls. Many people visit to enjoy the peace and see butterflies, birds and wildflowers, deep in the heart of the city. Little patches of countryside within a city, like this, are vitally important for both wildlife and people.

Get this!

Don't tidy up your garden too much! Many small animals shelter among fallen leaves and branches and piles of logs.

Glossary

adapted when a living thing has special features that allow it to survive in its particular habitat. For example, whales have blubber to keep them warm in cold water.

algae plants without leaves, roots, stems or flowers that can make their own food by photosynthesis

amphibian animal that lives on land and in water at different stages during its life

antennae pair of feelers on an insect's head used to feel or taste

bird of prey bird that hunts animals for food

breed when a male and female animal have babies

camouflage colours and patterns that help hide an animal's body against its background

carbon dioxide gas in the air around us

carnivores animals that eat other animals

conservation taking action to protect plants, animals and wild habitats

food web diagram that shows how food energy is passed on from plants to animals

habitat place where plants and animals live

herbivore animal that eats plants

hibernate to go into a very deep sleep during cold weather

insect small six-legged animal which, when adult, have bodies divided into three sections: head, thorax (chest) and abdomen (stomach)

larvae young stage in life cycle of some animals, between hatching from an egg and becoming an adult

lichen small, plant-like organism often found on bare rocks. Lichen is a mixture of algae and fungus growing together.

mammal type of animal group with some hair. Female mammals can give birth to live young, which they feed on their own milk.

migrate when animals regularly move from one place to another and back again. Many animals stay in one place in summer and migrate to another for winter.

native living naturally in a particular place

nectar sweet liquid some plants make to attract animal pollinators

nocturnal active at night

nutrient kind of chemical found in soil or in food that nourish plants and animals

oxygen gas in the air that animals breathe in and which living things need to survive

parasite organism that lives on and takes its food from another organism

pest an annoying or harmful insect or other animal

photosynthesis process by which plants make their own food using water, carbon dioxide and energy from sunlight

pollinate when pollen from the male part of a plant combines with an ovule (egg) in the female part of a plant to form seeds

pollution when chemicals or waste escapes into the air, water or soil and damages the habitat there for living things

predator animal that catches and eats other animals

prey animal that is caught and eaten by another animal

proboscis long tube-like mouth that some insects use to suck up liquid food

reptile egg-laying animal, such as a lizard, with scaly skin that usually lives on land

rodent type of mammal, with long tail, clawed feet and teeth for gnawing

sap sugary liquid food inside a plant's stem

scavengers animals that feed on dead plant or animal material

species group of living things that are similar in many ways and can breed together

spores plants such as ferns and mosses that release spores to grow into new plants

urban found in towns and cities

waxy natural, plastic-like layer over leaves or fruit on plants

wetland area of land that is always wet, such as bog

Find out more

Books

Garden Wildlife (Collins Nature Guides), Michael Chinery (Collins, 1997)

Kingfisher Handbook of the Wildlife of Britain and Europe (Kingfisher Facts and Records), Jeanette Harris (Kingfisher, 1998)

The Wildlife Trusts Handbook of Garden Wildlife, Nicholas Hammond (The Wildlife Trusts, 2002)

A Year in the Life of a Wildlife Garden, Jenny Steel (Webbs Barn Designs, 2001)

Websites

The Wildlife Trusts website has information about UK urban wildlife, location of reserves and news: www.wildlifetrusts.org

http://www.wildlife-gardening.co.uk/ has information about making a wildlife garden

You can find out about what native plants live in your area by typing in your postcode at: www.nhm.ac.uk/science/projects/fff

Many national and international conservation groups work to protect town and city habitats and wildlife, for example Friends of the Earth (www.foe.co.uk) and the Worldwide Fund for Nature (www.wwf-uk.org). Find out about more local groups in your nearest library.

Index